CW00693841

# SPIRIT OF **PADSTOW**

**ROBIN JONES**

First published in Great Britain in 2010


All pictures by Robin Jones



British Library Cataloguing-in-Publication Data
A CIP record for this title is available from the British Library

ISBN 978 0 85710 028 3

**PiXZ Books**
Halsgrove House, Ryelands Industrial Estate,
Bagley Road, Wellington, Somerset TA21 9PZ
Tel: 01823 653777
Fax: 01823 216796
email: sales@halsgrove.com

An imprint of Halstar Ltd, part of the Halsgrove group of companies
Information on all Halsgrove titles is available at: www.halsgrove.com

Printed and bound in China by Toppan Leefung Printing Ltd

# Introduction

Those 'in the know' will for decades have been familiar with the unique charm of Padstow, a traditional Cornish slate country fishing port that provides a dramatic contrast with bustling brash Newquay 12 miles down the coast.

However, it was the installation in 1990 of harbour gates which for the first time allowed round-the-clock deep water mooring for visiting yachts and other large pleasure craft that really began its transformation into today's fashionable and upmarket resort.

While many changes have taken place over the two decades that followed, Padstow remains remarkably unspoiled, and thanks to the great care taken by residents old and new, has been able to tastefully graft the old with the new.

Therefore we have designer boutiques, surf shops, art galleries and the restaurant empire of the town's celebrity TV chef Rick Stein rubbing shoulders with a tradition that dates back to pagan times: Padstow's famous 'Obby Oss' festival on May 1, not so long ago a decidedly local affair but one which now attracts visitors from all over the globe.

I have been visiting Padstow for a third of a century, and yet still manage to discover something new and magical each time.

To John and Sheila Lees, who discovered Padstow in the fifties

PAOLO SOPRANI

## PADSTOW MAY DAY SONG

*Unite and unite and let us all unite,*
*For summer is acome unto day,*
*And whither we are going we will all unite,*
*In the merry morning of May.*
*Arise up Mr......... I know you well afine,*
*For summer is acome unto day,*
*You have a shilling in your purse and I wish it was in mine*
*In the merry morning of May.*
*All out of your beds,*
*For summer is acome unto day,*
*Your chamber shall be strewed with the white rose*
*and the red,*
*In the merry morning of May.*
*Where are the young men that here now should dance,*
*For summer is acome unto day,*
*Some they are in England and some they are in France*
*In the merry morning of May.*
*Where are the maidens that here now should sing*
*For summer is acome unto day,*
*They are in the meadows the flowers gathering,*
*In the merry morning of May.*
*Arise up Mr...... with your sword by your side,*
*For summer is acome unto day,*
*Your steed is in the stable awaiting for to ride*
*In the merry morning of May.*
*Arise up Miss and strew all your flowers,*
*For summer is acome unto day,*
*It is but a while ago since we have strewed ours*
*In the merry morning of May.*

*Chorus*
*O! where is St. George, O, where is he O?*
*He is out in his long-boat all on the salt sea O.*
*Up flies the kite and down falls the lark O,*
*Aunt Ursula Birdhood she had an old ewe,*
*And she died in her own Park O.*

The Padstow 'Obby Osses' emerge from their stables on the morning of May 1 and return by midnight. An ancient fertility rite, some believe that the festivities date back to Iron Age times and may be linked to a forgotten religion which venerated horses. One legend says it began with Trevelyan, the only person who escaped the drowning of the legendary kingdom of Lyonesse in an earthquake by fleeing the inrushing sea on a black horse.

With its teaser in front, the Red Ribbon Oss gyrates towards the quayside.

The Red Ribbon Oss party leaving Prideaux Place, the manor house of Padstow.

Above: Blue Ribbon Oss flags flying high. Followers of the original Obby Oss wear red neckscarves: the Blue Oss, or Peace Oss, whose followers wear blue ones, is a 'recent' tradition introduced after World War One.

Right: Marking the return of spring, boughs of greenery from local woods are fixed in place around the town.

The Blue Ribbon Oss outside Padstow's biggest hotel, the four-star Metropole, which opened when the North Cornwall Railway arrived in 1899 bringing visitors from London.

O B
B

Opposite: The Oss twists and turns as he is led through the streets, egged on by a 'teaser' and accompanied by a band of musicians playing the Day Song. The pagan hobby horse tradition, which also survives in Minehead, Somerset, marks the Celtic festival of Beltane.

Right: Leading each Obby Oss procession is a master of ceremonies dressed in top hat and tails.

A Padstow boutique displaying traditional May Day attire, white shirts, blouses or jumpers with matching trousers and a blue or red sash and neckerchief, depending on which Oss you are following, and Obby Oss masks decorate a shop window.

The Blue Ribbon Oss is led along a packed South Quay.

The harbour is packed with visiting boats who have tied bunting to their masts for May Day. Street hawkers display their wares by the quayside.

A Red Ribbon Oss reveller enjoys a grandstand view from the top of the entrance gate at Prideaux Place.

Left: Each round of the May Song ends with the followers shouting: "Oss Oss wee Oss!"

Below: Symbolising death and rebirth, at intervals the Oss falls to the ground as the chorus of the May Song is sung, then rises again to loud cheers.

Patriotic fervour: the Cornish flag, recalling the times when the duchy was an independent Celtic kingdom, is displayed on May 1.

Left: Each procession ends up at the maypole in the town centre before the Oss returns to its stable. An Oss weathervane sits on top.

The London Inn, a splendid traditional pub in Lanadwell Street.

The Shipwright's Arms on North Quay once had two shipyards operating nearby, with a large saw pit outside its front door where timber was cut to size.

Left: This railway milepost preserved outside the Shipwright's Arms marks the fact that Padstow was 259 miles from London's Waterloo by train.

The Old Custom House Inn on South Quay occupies a former office of the revenue men as the name suggests, along with another old grain warehouse.

Right: Formerly known as the Commercial Hotel, the seventeenth-century Harbour Inn is the stable of the Blue Ribbon Oss.

The Golden Lion in Lanadwell Street
is the home of the Red Ribbon Oss.

Left: The Old Ship Hotel in Mill Square.

King of all he surveys, with a never-ending appetite: the town crier of Padstow!

Opposite: The outlines of a trio of trawlers cast their reflections on the waters of the inner harbour.

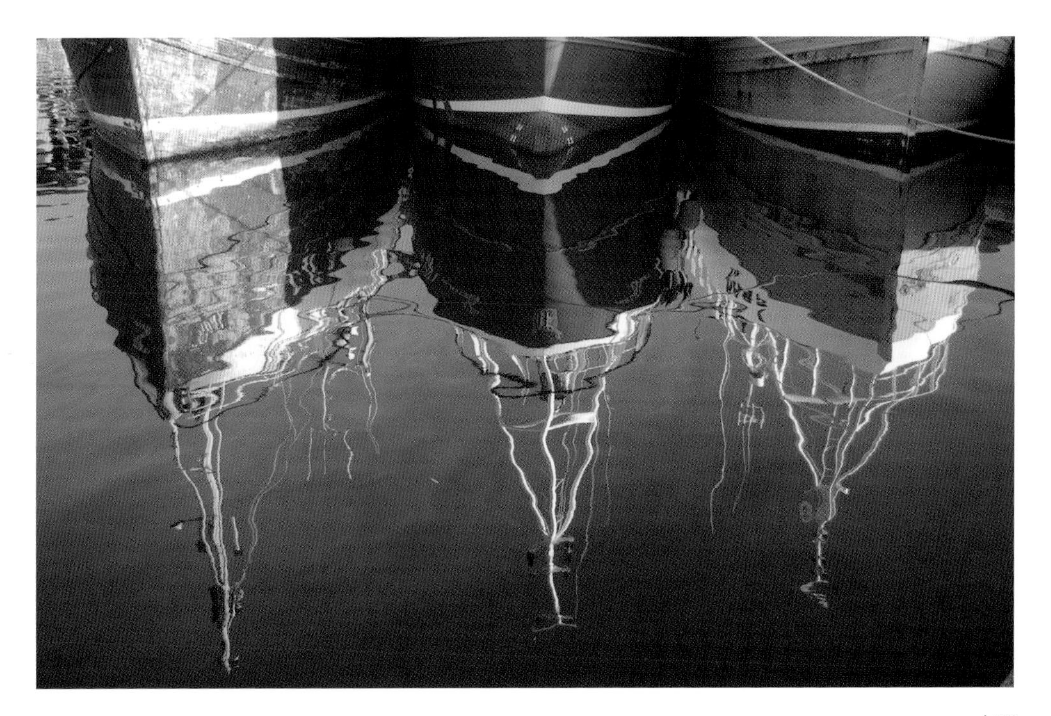

Padstow Harbour, as seen from South Quay. Since the early nineties, the harbour has been protected by gates which retain water levels at high tide, allowing large vessels like yachts to berth.

Early morning sunshine catches the harbour at its finest. Padstow is renowned for its deep azure skies, often referred to as the 'Padstow Blue' effect.

Left: The focal point of Padstow Harbour is the Red Brick Building, a warehouse structure typical of East Anglia but unique in Cornwall. The original warehouse of 1970, built with locally-baked bricks, was pulled down in 1990 and rebuilt, to the same design, as private flats, a boat store and the town's Tourist Information Office.

Opposite: Dawn breaks over the sleeping harbour at the start of another superb August day.

THE HARBOUR SHOP

The Victorian and Regency buildings on North Quay are built into the sheer rock face of the scarp which surrounds the harbour.

The South Quay: Victorian and Georgian warehouses have long been converted to shops with holiday flats above.

Opposite: The outer harbour at North Quay at low tide.

Padstow's own pleasure cruiser, the *Jubilee Queen*, which offers trips both out to sea and up the Camel Estuary, stands high and dry during a rare period out of season when the inner dock was emptied for maintenance.

Regular Sunday afternoon concerts are given on Padstow's harbourside bandstand by local brass bands and choirs.

Rick Stein's world famous Seafood Restaurant in Riverside.

Many visitors today immediately associate Padstow with TV celebrity chef Rick Stein who now owns several establishments in the town, from a fish and chip restaurant to cafés and St Petroc's Hotel in New Street and even a seafood school!

Opposite: Prideaux Place, the castellated Elizabethan manor house on the hill above Padstow, has been home to the Prideaux and Prideaux-Brune family for nearly five centuries. The future Charles II is said to have stayed there after fleeing to France from his defeat at the Battle of Naseby in 1645. The owners welcome the 'Ossing' parties into the grounds every May Day.

Right: Medieval Abbey House on North Quay is Padstow's oldest building and is said to have a secret tunnel leading beneath the hill to Prideaux Place.

The parish church of St Petroc which dates from Norman times, although most of the present structure is fifteenth century.

The Memorial Hall in Riverside was built after World War One and often houses displays of local paintings and collectors' fairs.

Left: A stained glass window depicting St George, one of the characters mentioned in the chorus of the Padstow May Song.

Dating from 1875, this grouping of cottages off Middle Street was built for the widows of sea captains, many of who set out from Padstow never to return.

Marble Arch in Church Street with its overhanging slate-hung room has a public right-of-way passage running through it.

The slate-hung Chough Bakery in The Strand.

Padstow as a centre for art galleries is becoming a rival to St Ives.

Left: One of Padstow's longest-serving souvenir shops, the Shell Shop specialises in exotic shells from around the world.

The National Lobster Hatchery which stands on the docks aims is to help maintain a healthy lobster population in Cornwall through conservation, education and research, and includes a visitor centre where you can see baby lobsters.

Opposite: Padstow, once the westernmost extremity of the Southern Railway, was served by trains from 1899 until January 1967. The station is now the town council's offices.

Ladies
Gentlemen
HELP

The iconic surfers' vehicle, the sixties Volkwagen camper van, examples of which can always be seen around Padstow, inspired this porcelain ornament in a town centre shop window.

Left: An obvious commodity in a town surrounded by some of the best beaches in Britain.

Traditional Cornish fare aplenty on sale.

Left: The Fo'c'sle Restaurant on North Quay is one of Padstow's longest-established.

Chapel Stile at the northern end of the town recreation ground takes the coastal footpath from Padstow onward to Hawker's Cove. In the Middle Ages a chapel dedicated to St Saviour stood at this point.

Opposite: The Padstow to Rock ferry across the estuary of the River Camel was authorised by Edward the Black Prince, in his role as Duke of Cornwall, in 1337, and was previously known as Black Rock or Tor Ferry.

Left: The Celtic-style memorial to the men of Padstow who lost their lives in two world wars.

Opposite: Padstow viewed from its sister settlement of Rock on the far side of the Camel.

Padstow as seen from the recreation ground shortly after summer sunrise.
The three-span curved girder railway bridge stands in the distance to the left.

Above: Preserved on the ridge of the roof of Barclay's Bank in Duke Street are two earthenware figures of horsemen, probably dating from medieval times when they indicated a change of horses could be obtained. A local story says that on the stroke of midnight, they once came alive and galloped around the nearby Market Place.

Right: The restored town pump in Fentonluna Lane which dates from 1592 was sited near an early Christian holy well that existed in the sixth century when the Celtic missionary St Petroc founded Padstow, formerly known as Lodenek.

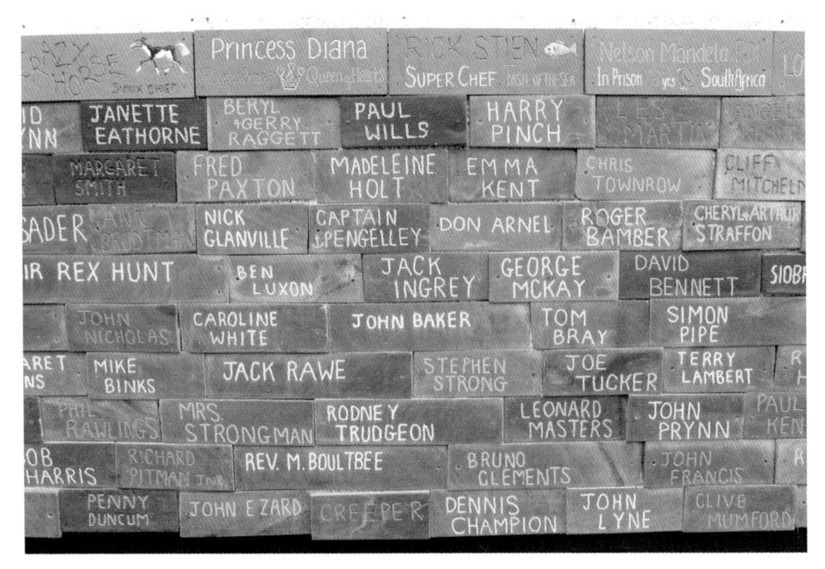


Padstow man Ed Prynn has created his own modern-day megalithic stone circle in the garden of his bungalow near the town and holds druidic ceremonies there.
Above: The names of the rich and famous who have visited Ed Prynn's famous stone circle.

To cross Little Petherick Creek on the approach to Padstow, the London & South Western Railway built this unique three-span girder bridge on a curve. It now carries the Camel Trail. Above it on Dennis Hill stands the 50ft-high Jubilee Monument, erected in 1887 in honour of Queen Victoria.

Opposite: The Camel Trail which uses the old railway trackbed between Padstow, Wadebridge, Bodmin and Bodmin Moor is one of Britain's most popular cyclepaths because of the stunning views over the estuary.

The sandbank across the mouth of the Camel Estuary known appropriately as the Doombar is second only to the Goodwin Sands in the English Channel in terms of danger and casualties to shipping. It was said to have been created by the dying curse of a mermaid killed by a Padstow fisherman.

Opposite: The sailing resort of Rock lies on the far side of the Camel Estuary, with the Padstow beach of Hawker's Cove in the foreground.

Hawker's Cove at high tide, a few minutes walk from the town centre. At low tide, it gives way to a massive expanse of sand; backed by dunes and sheltered from the Atlantic winds, it quickly becomes a suntrap with plenty of safe bathing in very shallow water.

Opposite: Beyond the Doombar, the waves of the Atlantic meet the waters of the Camel Estuary, with Pentire Point and Newlands Island in the distance, as viewed from Stepper Point.

Harbour Cove to the north of Padstow. To the left is the redundant original lifeboat station: on the right are cottages, one of which was owned by the late TV actor Edward Woodward, star of *Callan* and The *Equaliser*, who died in 2009.

The hollow 40ft high stone tower known as the Daymark stands above Stepper Point and was built as a guide to mariners entering the estuary and crossing the dreaded Doombar. It stands near the site of an Iron Age camp.

The breathtaking view of the Atlantic Ocean from the Daymark,
looking eastwards up the North Cornwall coast.

Opposite: Harvest time view of Rock and Daymer Bay on the far side the Camel Estuary.

Because of the danger presented by crossing the Doombar, Padstow's modern-day lifeboat station is located at Mother Ivey's Bay four miles to the west.

Right: A short walk from the Daymark is Pepper Hole, one of several local 'round holes' caused by the collapse of a cave through wave erosion.